How To Get A Job In The Film Industry

How To Get A Job In The Film industry
by
Cameron M. Burns

A Unique Guide To Getting Started In Hollywood

Hard-Pressed Books
P.O. Box 1925
Basalt, CO 81621
USA

Published by
Hard-Pressed Books
P.O. Box 1925
Basalt, CO 81621

First edition, 1998

Manufactured in the United States of America.

Edited by Kerry L. Burns and Mary J. Burns.
Book design by Ann Elizabeth Burns and Sylvia B. Robertson.
Cover Design by Lefty Angus Burns.
Technical Direction by Bob Robertson.

Front Cover photograph by Cameron M. Burns
Back Cover: The author standing in for Bruce Campbell on the set of "Sundown," Moab, Utah, 1989. Photo: Burns collection.

Library of Congress Cataloging-In-Publication Data

Burns, Cameron M.
    How To Get A Job In The Film Industry/Cameron M. Burns

ISBN: 0-9629627-0-8

Advertisers: If you would like to advertise in the next edition of "How To Get A Job In The Film Industry," contact Hard-Pressed Books, P.O. Box 1925, Basalt, CO 81621.

Watch for other titles in Hard-Pressed Books' "Get A Job!" Series coming soon to a bookseller near you.

*For **Ethan Putterman**, for all the crazy, wonderful, spontaneous madness he inspired in my life.*

The camera: Photo by Cameron M. Burns.

Contents

Acknowledgements

This book would not have come together without help from numerous people. First and foremost, my family: Mary, Kerry and Gillian Burns; Bob and Sylvia Robertson; Penny, Mike, Jessica, Natalie and Katie Sandy.

Film guru Dennis Junt and his family, Jordan, Zach and Theresa, treated me as if I was one of the family for all my years in Hollywood, and I thank them for their kindness.

Chris Pomeroy, of the Carbondale-based Lapdog Productions, gave me invaluable help during the final stages of book design. Kay Stevens, of Thomson-Shore also gave me a great deal of assistance, which I appreciate.

Lefty Angus Burns is my black lab/shepherd mix, and he provided incredible encouragement, as well as technical assistance throughout the production of this book.

Also, thanks to Chuck and Suzanne Brown; Steve, Sandy, Tori and Angelo Porcella; Iris, Walden and Talia Putterman; Mike and Claire Schillaci; and my future publishing world colleagues, Bob and Elizabeth Ward.

My film mentors at the University of Colorado: Don Yannicito and Jerry Aronson, got me off on a weird path in life, and I'll never regret their guidance.

And, finally, a great big thank you to all the folks who agreed to star in my insane student movies: Ann Elizabeth Robertson Burns, Jeff O'Defey, Benny Bach, Doug Monsalud, Ingrid MacMillan, and the poor kitty with the busted up tail who lived near our basement in Boulder, Club Cat.

Preface

This book began as an idea in the late 1980s.

At that time, I had been crewing sporadically on feature films throughout the United States for three years, wandering, more or less, from state to state, production to production.

All the jobs I took on film crews were temporary, a month here, two months there, separated from each other by long climbing trips, to Mexico, the Sierra Nevada, wherever I felt like going.

Perhaps, because I was young, unmarried, with no children, and more interested in going climbing than working, I didn't care about my next job. While my fellow crew technicians were fretting over their next job, I would load up my gear and head off into the mountains for a month at a time.

But then I had a couple of lean times, when I couldn't get work crewing on movies, and the bills mounted. I knew a few tricks for getting jobs and began using them with resounding success. Some job-hunting tricks I developed myself, others I borrowed from friends I had observed in the chase for employment.

In 1991, in my then future wife's basement apartment in Boulder, I sat down and compiled my techniques into this manual, although it took another seven years for it to make it to press! Admittedly, this book is aimed at young people, who are more flexible and willing to take some chances, but I think anyone hoping to move into a career in the film or television industry can use the information within the pages.

Good luck and happy shooting!

Cam Burns

Basalt, Colorado, 1998

The typical film set is a mess of personnel, equipment and materials. Photo: Cameron M. Burns collection.

Chapter 1
INTRODUCTION

Hi. Welcome to "How to Get a Job in the Film Industry."

This book will be unlike any other How To book on employment that you will ever read. That's because the film and television industry is unlike any other business you'll ever be involved with.

This book is not about how to get a job as an actor or actress. This book is about getting a job, any job, behind the camera on a film or television crew. Certainly, some, if not most of the jobs in the entertainment industry are very UNglamorous, and some are downright awful. However, the film and television industry is extremely receptive to talent, and once you have gotten your foot in the door, almost anything is possible.

I know of one Hollywood producer who started as an extra and now oversees production of $12 million movies.

I know of one director, whose films have grossed over $100 million dollars, who got his break because he was working as an assistant director and the real director became ill. The film's producer asked him to complete the direction, and a career was born.

Success stories like these abound in Hollywood, and anyone with ambition, skill, brains and luck can have all the successes they want, as long as they are willing to persevere.

Perhaps the main reason the film and television industry is unlike any other business around is because the industry is chaotic.

The industry is chaotic because of the nature of filmmaking and, to a lesser extent, television production. Filmmakers and television producers must constantly move from place to place, set to set, to create a finished story that seems credible to the viewer. If you've ever watched someone filming a television commercial in your home town, you'll know that behind the camera is an unruly mess of equipment, personnel and materials.

Usually, the less expensive the production, the more anarchic the set and the organization of the production. But even big budget films, where chains of command are strictly adhered to, can, at times, take on the aura of a circus.

This ever-present chaos is not just a characteristic of the set, where the crew moves along at an often-frenzied pace in order to complete a set schedule of shooting. It is also characteristic of many film and television production offices, where managers and producers must move along planning and preparing all aspects of the production for the crew.

While most people in the film and television industry take the chaotic nature of filmmaking and television production for granted, and generally think nothing of it, this chaos allows the average individual to make easy, personal contact with film and television professionals in ways that no other industry allows.

That contact, making it and maintaining it, is what this book is all about.

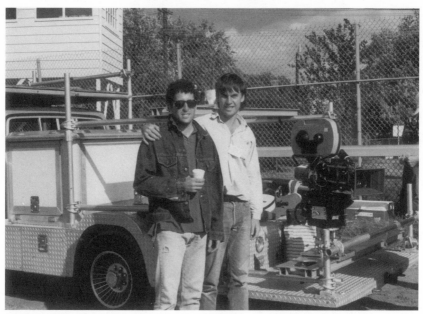

Making friends on the set. Photo: Cameron M. Burns collection.

Because the film business is so different from other industries, most of the techniques for getting a job described in this book will be quite different from the approaches you would normally use in trying to gain employment. I don't advocate simply dropping off resumes to producers, or production companies and praying for the best (although it does help to get your face and your resume in front of as many film production personnel as you can). Some of things I will describe to you will surprise you, maybe shock you, and hopefully make you laugh.

However, if you can use any of the tidbits you've read to get a job in the film industry, then I've done my job.

One of the greatest methods of self-advancement that people use is comparison. For this reason, I will rely heavily on narrating my own experiences to you. I have had a lot of good luck in finding jobs in the film industry, but I have also had, at times, bad luck. So, to help you figure out just how far you might go, or how far you have come, I will describe a few tricks I used to land jobs, and a few things I tried that didn't work. I hope, if nothing else, I can entertain.

Although I will describe methods of finding out about film productions close to where you live, methods of obtaining future film work, and other tips, there are innumerable tricks out there. It is important that you use your own creativity to get a job whenever you can.

If you read this guide and still have questions about trying to get a job in the film industry, you can often find plenty of advice at your local University and state film commission (for more on state film commissions, see Chapter 5-Sources for Employment). Also, look through your state or city's film and television production handbook (for more on production handbooks, see Chapter 5-Sources for Employment). Some professionals listed in these handbooks are willing to help individuals interested in working in the film industry.

Finally, check your local library or bookstore. In recent years, there have been a number of excellent guides published on film industry careers, although they do not address how to go about getting started in the industry.

Second unit personnel shooting special effects on an extremely low-budget horror movie. Photo: Cameron M. Burns.

Chapter 2
ABOUT THIS BOOK

This book is a guide for someone getting started in the film and/or television production business. It is about getting your first job on a film or television crew, not as an actor or actress.

It introduces the reader to a number of sources that can offer information about production companies that are hiring, both in your area of the United States, and in major cities.

In this book, several terms are used that all mean essentially the same thing. The term "film industry" generally applies to any situation where film or videotape is used to create a commercial film, national or local television program, advertisement, or promotional or industrial film. And the jobs that this book aims to help you get are generally not permanent positions. Most film crews work for an extended period of time. Anywhere from two weeks to four months is the norm. Then the crew members split up and go their separate ways once the final film or television program has been completed.

The most important thing about this book is that reading it alone cannot get you a job in the film industry. You must use this book as a tool, along with all the references in the back, to find employment.

Many of you who have already worked in the film industry will likely know how to go about getting another job in film or television production, and have contacts. Still, this book can be handy as it contains a large supply of references of which you might be unaware.

Physically, this book is laid out like a story.

It begins with a brief description of what actually takes place on a film set (Chapter 3-The Filmmaking Process), the moment to moment, day-to-day, and week-to-week activities of a film crew. How a shooting schedule is prepared, how sets are located, how the action is rehearsed and then filmed. From this description, you can learn exactly what each task a crew member of a film or television production performs. Once you have an idea of what everyone does, you might have a better understanding of the type of position you would like to work towards getting on a film crew.

After that, there is an in depth guide to starting out, (Chapters 4, 5, 6 and 7); trying to move into the film industry if you've never worked in Hollywood before.

Personal contact is the single most important aspect of getting work in the film industry. Who you know is essential. Hollywood is NOT an equal opportunity employer! I'll give you a few tips on how and where to meet a few

15

good contacts for work in the film industry.

The most important thing about film work other than getting your first job is maintaining a flow of work. How to go about keeping yourself employed in the movies is described in Chapter 8-Maintaining a Steady Flow of Work.

In Chapter 9, I'll describe some of the opportunities available to you through your community's colleges and universities, and how you might use these to break into the film industry.

Then I'll give you a couple of tips on positive personal traits that all

Simon Wincer (foreground) directing a horse race scene in the mini-series "Bluegrass," 1987. Photo by Cameron M. Burns.

employers, not just producers and production managers, look for when hiring someone (Chapter 10).

The back of this book is comprised of several large appendices that will be infinitely valuable to you if you're just starting out. It is these appendices that make this book a handy reference tool that you will likely use over and over again.

Appendix A gives an in-depth description of what kind of jobs are available on a movie crew; what the First A.D. (assistant director) does, what the gaffer does, that sort of thing.

Appendix B lists the State Film Production Offices for every state in the entire U.S. The people who run these offices will know everything about films being shot in their state and are a valuable source of information to tap.

Appendix C lists the vital statistics for the two best Hollywood trade magazines that print statistics on films being shot in the U.S. and abroad each and every week. And finally, Appendix D lists several websites as of March, 1998 that list jobs in the film industry.

You can use this book anyway you want. (My wife used one copy of the manuscript to hold up one corner of a wobbly kitchen table). But I thoroughly recommend reading as much of it as possible before you flip to the appendices in the back of the book and start making random phone calls.

Film Job Fact: In 1996, the average feature film cost $39.8 million to produce, and $19.8 million to market.

The typical close up shot. Photo by Cameron M. Burns.

Chapter 3
THE FILMMAKING PROCESS

Lights! Camera! Action! You've probably heard these expressions hundreds of times. Does it leave you wondering what exactly takes place on the average film or television set? How is a film made? What is a gaffer? What does a foley artist do? Answers to a few of these questions are in this chapter where I describe the filmmaking process. In doing so, I will explain some of the jobs held by members of a film crew. However, a more complete and in-depth description of the various film crew positions will be given in Appendix A (Film Crew Positions) at the back of the book.

Any film, ranging from a Hollywood feature to a public television station documentary begins with an idea. And, if you've seen a lot of movies you'll realize that a lot of the ideas that instigated the movie making process were horrible. Whether the film is the concept of a producer, director, writer, or just a regular guy on the street, all movies begin in the mind.

From that point, a film can go one of several directions.

If the person with the film idea is a well-connected film industry professional, then usually they will try to sell the movie idea, long before a script is even written. Once they have sold the concept to a studio or distribution company, the person with the idea will have enough money to hire a screenwriter.

If the person with the idea has no money or Hollywood connections, he or she must write a script and try and sell the script,an impossible task at best. There are very few people who succeed using this route, but occasionally a few persistent inviduals do manage to sell their scripts.

Anyway, let's suppose a film has been sold, then written, or written then sold, and it is going to be produced. Then, usually the film's executive producer, the guy who did the selling and now has the money to make the movie, hires a producer. The executive producer may also hire the director, or the executive producer and producer may hire the director together. Once these "key" people have been hired, a few other "keys" are hired such as the production designer, art director, first assistant director, editor, and cinematographer. The unit production manager, or production manager is also hired around this time. The actors are usually hired before the key people, but occasionally an actor may not have committed himself to the film until the day before shooting!

The Production Office

After some key hirings have been made, a production office is set up close to where the bulk of the filming is to take place. Sometimes these produc-

19

tion offices are in rented hotel rooms, sometimes they're in empty warehouses in the San Fernando Valley (Los Angeles).   Wherever they're set up, production offices become the base from which the film crew members work.

For you and your search to get a job working in the film industry, the setting up of a production office is the most important aspect in the filmmaking process. That's because once a production office is set up, it means that a film has been funded by someone, and barring any financial disasters for those who are funding the film, it will actually be made. It also means that the producers will undoubtedly be hiring film crew members. (For more information on production offices, see "The State Film Office" in Chapter 5.)

Usually, at about this point in the process, the director will go over the script and break it down into a shooting schedule with the first assistant director ("first A.D."). They put all the similar scenes together. Obviously, it makes sense to shoot all the scenes that have the same location, actors, and special effects, at the same time. This cuts production costs immensely. For instance, if there are two car chase scenes in a film, the producer will usually hire a stuntman for two or three days, shoot the car chase scenes on consecutive days, then release the stuntman from the production. Were the film crew to shoot the car chase scenes in chronological order, the stuntman may work one day, then do nothing for two months, until the crew reaches the second car chase in the story. By shooting similar scenes out of order, a producer can save money and the stuntman's time.

The One Line Schedule

Once the shooting schedule has been prepared, the first A.D. usually prepares what's called a one line schedule, which is just a shorter version of the descriptions in the shooting schedule. One day's worth of filming is generally about four pages long in a shooting schedule whereas in a one line schedule there is about a day and a half's worth of filming on each page. It helps the director and assistant directors know what's coming up without having to wade through reams of paper.

Once the shooting schedule has been prepared, the director will go out to scout locations for shooting. Usually, the art director, first A.D. and cinematographer go with the director. They will be working at these locations so the more that they can learn about them the better off they'll be when shooting begins. Scouting locations usually takes between one and four weeks, but as with everything in the film industry, nothing is standardized.

Often, while the director has been scouting locations, the producer and/or unit production manager has been hiring many of the film crew members who aren't as high up as the key people. They may have been busy hiring the gaffer, electricians, grips, carpenters, make-up artists, special effects artists, stuntmen, second assistant directors, production assistants, and so on. About a week or two after the locations have been picked and the shooting schedule completed, filming will commence. And, surprisingly, it is quite often during this week before shooting begins that many of the actors commit themselves to the film. There are so many actors in Hollywood that finding someone to play a specific role is usually easier than finding a good special effects artist.

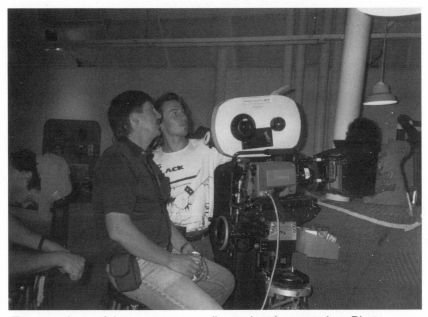

Two members of the camera crew discussing the next shot. Photo: Cameron M. Burns collection.

Then the shooting begins. The first day of filming on any production is usually pretty awkward and hectic as the different departments in the crew learn to work efficiently with one another.

The first event on any day's shooting is getting the crew members to the location. If the film is an "in town" shoot, meaning that the film is being shot in Los Angeles, then most often the crew members commute to the set under their own means. They drive their own vehicles or car pool as they would for any other job. If the film is being shot on location, say in Alaska or the hills of South Dakota, then the production company provides transportation for the crew from their hotel rooms to the set. This is usually in the form of a mini-van or a group of mini-buses.

Making A Scene

Once the crew has arrived at the set, work begins. The day's shooting has already been planned and is printed on a call sheet. Generally whole scenes or large portions of scenes are shot at one particular time. The first step towards beginning the day's shooting is lighting the scene. This is a straightforward process. The director will rehearse the scene with the actors, while the cinematographer is present. It is essential that the cinematographer be present during rehearsals as he will need to know what the actors will be doing during each shot. After all he must make sure that light falls upon the actors throughout the shot, or, as I'm sure you've seen in some horror movies, the cinematographer might want to keep some actors in the dark. Whatever the case, the first step to shooting a scene is rehearsing the action with the cinematographer present.

Once the cinematographer (the cinematographer is sometimes called the "D.P.," short for director of photography) has watched the rehearsal, the actors leave the set. They are usually sent to make-up, where their hair will be styled and their faces made up. The make-up process takes a great deal of time, so it is usually commenced as soon as the actors have been through a rehearsal.

Back on the set, the cinematographer instructs the gaffer as to the exact lighting arrangement he will use. The gaffer, in turn, orders his electricians to start "running" cable throughout the set and setting up the lights. Running cable and setting lamps is one of the most difficult aspects of any film production. The equipment is cumbersome, awkward and very dangerous to handle. It is surprising to many people that most electricians who work in the film industry need not have any sort of license or certificate to work with electricity. The electricians will also place numerous three-pin AC outlets (regular domestic outlets) around the set so that other members of the crew can plug their electrical appliances into a power source. An example of other crew members requiring power would be the make-up artist needing a hair dryer on the set to dry an actors hair, or the special effects team may require an outlet to run a fogger (a device that creates thick clouds that drift close to the ground).

Tag Teams

Once the cable infrastructure has been laid down, the second team are brought onto the set. The second team, put purely and simply, is made up of stand-ins. The first team are the actors. Although most people think that stand-ins are used primarily during a dangerous shot, or in the case that the lead actor may get hurt, this is far from true. The most important function of a stand-in comes during the setting up of the lights. Stand-ins are often required to stand for literally hours on end while the cinematographer gets the lighting perfect. A long time ago in Hollywood some famous actor decreed that standing around while the electricians pointed their lights and added colored gels was beneath him, so he hired someone else to stand in his place until the lights were ready. The tradition lives on and many stand-ins have made lifetime careers "standing-in" for actors whom they resemble.

The stand-ins are brought to the set by the assistant directors. The assistant directors coordinate the human aspect of the film crew: the make-up of the lead actors, the crowd scenes, the wardrobe personnel, and other actor-related aspects of the filmmaking process. The cinematographer, on the other hand, coordinates the technical aspects of the filmmaking process: the lighting, electricity, the camera movements, and other "technical" items.

Shooting a promotional video. Photo by Lefty Angus Burns.

Getting Tweaked

So the stand-ins are brought to the set where they stand, usually for a long time while the electricians and grips "tweak" the lights until they are perfect. The grips set up "flags" to block out portions of light that are distracting or unneeded, They also set up screens that diffuse the light, and bounce cards, large white pieces of cardboard that bounce light onto the actors. Meanwhile the electricians add or remove gels and scrims to the lights that they have set up. Gels are sheets of colored plastic that are placed in front of the lights to produce color, while scrims are steel meshes that are placed in front of the bulb, inside the light itself, that cut down the light even more than a screen. Basically, scrims, screens and gels are different light altering tools.

The whole time that the grips and electricians are making the set a perfectly lit environment for filming, the camera crew is preparing the camera. This means that each member of the camera crew will be doing different tasks in preparation for the upcoming shot. The second assistant cameraman is busy loading magazines with film. A film truck is almost always a feature of any film crews vehicular entourage. It contains a darkroom right in the back of the truck where the second assistant cameraman can change film.

Maintaining Focus

Meanwhile, the first assistant cameraman is busy practicing "focus pulling" and setting marks on the floor. "Focus-pulling" and "racking focus" are two expressions that mean the same thing and are often used on a film set. When a scene is being shot, often the actors walk from a point that is, say, ten feet from the camera, to a point that is three feet from the camera. If this sequence is shot as one movement (one single shot) then it will be necessary for the first assistant cameraman to continually adjust the focus for the image to remain sharp. This is called pulling or racking focus. And, it is basically all that a first assistant cameraman does. He adjusts (or pulls, or racks) focus and not much else. It is one of the most important yet unknown jobs in the film industry. Without first assistant cameramen, nearly every actor in every film would have walked out-of-focus at some point.

To help him get the focus dead right, the first assistant cameraman places marks upon the floor or ground. These are usually little pieces of tape or rubber that sit flat upon the floor. Then, with a stand-in standing at the marks, the first assistant cameraman uses a tape measure to measure the distance from the camera's lens to the stand-in's nose. The focus ring on the camera's lens is calibrated to the exact measurements that are represented on the ring. Thus, by using his tape measure, the first assistant cameraman can get the actor perfectly in focus.

Moving Pictures

If the actor must move during the shot, the first assistant cameraman places a second mark on the floor to which the actor walks. He measures this second distance, from lens to actors nose, with his tape measure. Then, when the actor walks during the shot, the first assistant cameraman adjusts the focus from point A to point B. Usually the first assistant cameraman will use removable tape on the lenses' focus ring and mark it with a pen so that he can see the focus ring turning and estimate how smoothly he should twist. To make certain that the shot is in focus when filming begins, the camera crew rehearses the action with the stand-ins several times before the real actors are brought to the set.

While the first assistant cameraman is practicing focus-pulling, the key grip may practice moving the dolly, so that another movement is added to the shot. When dolly shots are being prepared, often dolly track is laid. This is done by the grips. When a new camera set-up is being prepared, the key grip stays with the camera to help the camera department support the actual camera. He readies the tri-pods, or boom arms or whatever apparatus the camera is to be mounted upon.

The whole time this is happening, the camera operator keeps his eye on the lens. On many films the camera operator's eye will be the only one that touches the eyepiece. The cinematographer might never look through the lens during the shooting of a film. On many films the director never looks through the lense, either. This may sound incredible, but the cinematographer's job is to oversee the lighting and the camera work on a shoot. If he has faith in the camera operator, he will often not bother looking through the lens. On the other hand, on extremely low-budget films, it's not uncommon to see the cinematographer working as camera operator as well as cinematographer. It all depends upon the crew, the film, and what's happening at the time. Remember, no two productions are alike.

Once the set has been lit, the camera crew has rehearsed focus-pulling, the key grip has practiced any dolly moves to be used, and the camera operator has made sure that the entire scene stays within the viewfinder, the actors and director are brought to the set.

Ready For Action

At this time the director will go over the shot with the actors. The actors are now made-up and have their hair done and are wearing their costumes. They will rehearse the action in the shot a few times before actually trying to capture the scene, or a portion of the scene, on film. When the director is pleased with the actors interpretation of the scene, he'll ask to shoot.

Now the first assistant director takes control, making sure that the entire location is quiet. The first A.D. will send the second assistant director to do "sound lock-up," if there are members of the crew that are likely to make noise during shooting. The assistant director department's production assistants are usually crucial during sound lock-up as they patrol certain sections of the location, letting everyone know when the filming has begun. Once everything is quiet, the first A.D. will call for the sound recordists to "roll sound." The sound recording device (usually a Nagra brand tape recorder) takes about a second to get up to its recording speed. Once it has gained that speed, the sound recordist lets the camera crew and everyone else know by saying "speed." Then the first A.D. will tell the camera crew to "roll camera." The second camera assistant then moves out in front of the camera with a clapboard, also known as a slate, sticks or marker. The second camera assistant says "mark", claps the clapboard, and moves quickly out of the way of the camera.

Now comes the moment for which everyone has been waiting. The crew is ready, the camera, or sometimes cameras, are rolling and the actors are in their places. Now the director gives his most famous of commands: "Action!" The actors do their thing, after which the director tells the entire crew "cut." If the director doesn't like anything about the way the action went - the actors expressions, the lighting, the special effects that were used in the shot

- he'll want to shoot it again. This brings us to takes.

Take That

Takes are simply the number of shots that are required to film that portion of the movie. Some shots are repeated twenty or thirty times. Some shots are perfect on their first go.

Once the film has been exposed and the sound reels are full, they are taken out of the camera by the second assistant cameraman and sound mixer, respectively, then given to one of the A.D.'s. The A.D. in turn makes sure that the newly shot film gets back to the production office where it is sent out by express courier to a laboratory, usually in Los Angeles or New York. The film crew, in the meantime, moves on to shoot the next scene according to their shooting schedule.

Charming Prints

After about two days the Lab has made two "prints" from the negative film and the sound roll. The sound print is basically a larger version of the original sound reel, enlarged to fit onto an editing deck. The image print is not the sort of print you would get from your neighborhood grocery store. It is 35mm clear print that can be projected. Think of it as a series of slides, all on one strip of film. In fact, the prints that are made in this portion of the filmmaking process are exactly the same thing as slides, they just haven't been cut down into individual frames.

The developed negative film, the prints from the negative, and the 35mm sound prints are then sent back to the film's production office. The editor and his assistants now take over. The original film negative is preserved, in case another print needs to be made from it, and the editor and his assistants, match the sound print to the image print. To do this, they use the clapboard or marker that was filmed at the beginning of each shot. By matching perfectly the image of the marker's sticks slapping together with the sound on the sound print, the editor can assure that the film will be "in-synch". You've probably seen old movies on television that are sometimes out of synch, the sound of the actors voices don't match their lips on the screen. This is because the editor didn't do his job properly. The sound and image prints weren't synchronized together correctly.

The Big Screening

After the image and sound have been synched together, the editor prepares them for a screening. While a crew is on location, these screenings occur every night after the crew has finished the days filming. Thus they are known as "dailies" or "rushes." They show film shot two to four days before, and by looking at dailies, a director can see if he wants to reshoot any of the film before the crew leaves that location. The cinematographer and actors often attend dailies; sometimes if the actors aren't pleased with their acting, or the cinematographer doesn't like his lighting, the director will be willing to reshoot that portion of the film.

The next day on the set will be about the same. The location and subject may have changed, but the routine will probably be about the same.

Post Production

The film, once it has been shot entirely, goes through a great deal of post production before it gets to the screen. After the crew members all go home, the director, producer and editors will often work for several months after shooting is complete, editing the final version of the film. Sound effects, laboratory visual effects and music are all added to make the raw footage the final product that the audience sees on the screen.

Film Job Fact: In the film "Braveheart" a white van can be seen driving through the back of one of the battle scenes. Normally, the assistant directors or off-duty police officers hired for the film's production would have the job of stopping traffic for a shot.

The resume dilemma. Photo by Lefty Angus Burns.

Chapter 4
STARTING OUT

So you have a boring job you don't like.

You want to work in an interesting business, and you think you'd like movie-making. You have no experience and no contacts.

Where do you start?

Creating A Film Industry Resume

There are a thousand ways to begin but the best thing to do first is prepare some kind of resume. This might sound scary, especially if you have absolutely nothing to write on a resume, but it's not as bad as it sounds and there are ways of making you look more attractive to a prospective employer. If nothing else, a resume lists your phone number and address, where a prospective production manager or producer can contact you. Even if you know nothing about filmmaking but show the type of attitude that production companies like, your resume can stand out because of your personality.

At first, your resume will undoubtedly be pretty pathetic, but as you get film industry jobs, each of those can be added so that even after a short time, your resume will be packed with employable experience.

One thing to watch out for is the perennial description of "purpose." In college, some students are taught to state their purpose for seeking a job. For example, "to direct motion pictures." Putting something as grandiose as your goal of directing on your resume will likely get your resume laughed into the production office trash recepticle as if you'd applied in drag.

Padding Your Resume

There are a few things that can help you pad your resume, so that it includes something film or television-related.

First, if you know nothing about filmmaking and want to work in the film industry, I highly recommend that you take basic filmmaking courses at your local university of community college. There is no set amount of course work you should take, but only take classes that emphasize film production or filmmaking.

Avoid taking film studies courses at universities and community colleges that focus on critical evaluation of a particular filmmaker's art (like a class on Alfred Hitchcock, for example). These critical classes will teach you either nothing or very little about the filmmaking process.

Filmmaking courses taught at unviersities and community colleges are

29

cheap, effective, and provide you with much information that will be helpful when you try and actually get a job in the film industry. (See Chapter 9- University Opportunities.)

Once you've take a few classes, those can go on your resume. Although it might sound like an ineffective tack, many producers appreciate prospective employees who are willing to go out and take classes in the field of their choice.

For those of you who know a lot about filmmaking from studying it, but have no actual experience, your classes, if you've learned your information in a formal class setting, can go on your resume. If you have ever worked on any kind of recorded production, from videotaping a wedding to preparing a school play, those should go on the resume. Anything that can or might be of interest to a film or television producer or production manager should go on your resume.

When it comes to organizing your resume, the best way to sell yourself is to list your "Film Production Experience" almost immediately on the first page, underneath personal information such as your telephone number, address, and social security number.

Another important thing to place on your resume is references. If you have any friends or relatives in the film or television business, add their names as references on your resume. This is especially important if you are applying for a job in a film or television market outside the major centers like Los Angeles and New York (Cincinnati, Atlanta, Denver, for example). Most people who work in these smaller markets know each other well, so a friend in the business will likely be known to all your potential employers.

"P.A. LAND"

As mentioned above, when making up your resume, you cannot simply write on it that you are a director or producer when trying to get your first job. You've got to aim low, or people in the industry won't take you seriously.

If you have no idea about what kind of job you'd like on a film or television set, or have absolutely no experience, even with student films, the best thing to write on your resume is "production assistant." Production assistants ("P.A.s") are the ultimate go-fers of the film industry. They do everything from getting coffee and donuts for the rest of the crew to minor construction projects to cleaning up an actor's puke. P.A.s get handed the most boring, most loathsome, most reviled jobs in the film industry. And all the while they are paid next to nothing. In fact, many producers and production managers expect you to work on your first film for free, just so you can break into the industry!

But for all the downsides to being a P.A., there are some important reasons why you will likely want to make becoming a P.A. your first goal in the film industry.

Number one, you don't need to know anything.

P.A.s are basically grunts who do what they're told. And if you've never worked on a film set, this is the best way to learn how it all goes together. Number two, these jobs are easiest to get.

A producer from Hollywood or New York who comes to your home town or state to shoot a movie will likely bring all his key people (director, art director, cinematographer, etc.) with him. Those people, in turn, will hire many of their key people (assistant directors, set designers, gaffers, etc.), who will in turn hire their friends to work for them. About the only positions left by the time the Great American Movie is set to shoot in Hometown, U.S.A., are P.A. positions.

Number three, opportunities always arise for P.A.s If you have half a brain on your shoulders (many people in Hollyweird don't) you can advance through the ranks and win a spot on another production by showing your willingness to work hard, by being punctual, and by solving minor problems yourself. My first job on a film crew at age 21, as a P.A., and by the time the film began shooting, the assistant directors on the crew had asked that I be a P.A. assigned to their department. By a few weeks into shooting, I was directing dozens of extras to create crowd scenes behind Mickey Rooney and Cheryl Ladd, who were getting their direction from the director.

It is important to realize that P.A.s never know where they'll end up. Many who apply for P.A. jobs thinking they'll be sitting next to Tom Cruise and refilling his coffee cup whenever it's low should think again.

If you are hired as a P.A., you might end up working at a production office, doing things that you'd do in an everyday office environment. You might never see the movie set. Or, if you get placed with the set construction crew painting backdrops for sets, you might see the set, but never anytime there's any filmmaking being done.

On many big productions, there will be dozens of P.A.s. Some will end up working for the whole production in the production office, and rarely see the set. Others might be given jobs taking care of actors and actresses for the entire production. Still others might be assigned to help the camera crew, or the electricians, or the grips. When you are a P.A., expect anything.

Producers and production managers often differntiate between P.A.s depending on whether or not they'll be working on the set or not. If you can, try to get a job as a "set P.A."

P.A.s who don't work on the set miss most of the thrill of production. However, you might have to work one or two jobs as a non-set P.A. before you get the opportunity of being allowed to work on the set.

Even if you land a job as a set P.A., you can never know exactly where you'll end up on a set. I worked as a P.A. on a half dozen films early in my film industry career. Once as a P.A. for the camera crew, once as a P.A. for the grips, once as a P.A. for the production coordinator and several times as a P.A. for the assistant directors.

As a set P.A., it's most likely that you will end up working for the assistant directors, running various errands on and around the set and telling everyone to shut up when the film starts rolling.

Besides learning how a film crew functions, or doesn't function, as the case may be, and getting some real experience for your resume, one other benefit of working as a P.A. is that you will make contacts with those already in the film industry. Often, if other film crew members like you, they will ask you to come and work in their part of the industry. After working on one film in Kentucky for the assistant directors, I was asked to work on a subsequent film in New York by members of the camera crew. I had gotten along with them well, and once the Kentucky film ended, they wanted me to go to New York and work as a camera P.A, loading magazines, taking care of lenses, that sort of thing. I declined the offer, but the point is simple: If you are intrested in a certain aspect of film production, being a P.A. on your first production can help you get there.

It's likely that 70 percent of those who are offered jobs on a film, television or advertisement production will become P.A.s on their first job.

The P.A. position, by its very nature, allows you to observe the entire filmmaking process. If you start out with no great expectations, show you're a good, intelligent, worker, anything can happen. There's no way you can show up at a film production office and ask to direct the company's next feature film with Arnold Schwarzenegger and Sylvester Stallone.

Cheap Labor?

One common technique for acquiring cheap labor, that many producers and production managers have turned to, is to not pay P.A.s, in return for experience on a real shoot, or a promise that you will be hired on the producer's next big money film.

Taking a non-paying P.A. job is entirely up to you, but I would recommend against it, unless you absolutely don't have to worry about paying the bills at home.

First, there are enough paying P.A. jobs out there if you're willing to hustle and find one, and filmmakers who don't pay P.A.s are just sleazy and cheap. After all, P.A.s are the cheapest part of any production.

Second, don't base any career decisions you might make on promises from a Hollywood film person. These promises are about as flimsy as an ocean yacht made out of typing paper. More than likely, the guy making the promise doesn't even have the wherewithal to back up the promise.

If you do jump in and work for free, make sure your expenses (especially car mileage) is paid for by the production company, and try to get some college credit for the hours you put in. Many universities and community colleges can offer credit for someone working in the film industry.

Sending out your resume.

Surprising to most neophyte film and television industry hopefuls, there are hundreds of places where you can take your resume.

There are three places you should target immediately:

1. Your state's film office or commission;

2. Local and state film and television production companies; and

3. Out-of-state production companies who are shooting films, televsion programs or advertisements in your area.

These three sources for film industry work, and why they are so important to your getting started in the industry, are described in the next chapter, Sources for Employment.

Film Job Fact: In 1989, the average Production Assistant working in Hollywood made $250-350 per week. In 1989, "Batman" grossed $251.2 million.

State production handbooks. These manuals vary in style, format and size for every state and province in North America. Handbooks for Missouri, Mississippi, Prince Edward Island (Canada), and Alaska are shown. Photo by Cameron M. Burns.

Chapter 5
SOURCES FOR EMPLOYMENT

There are three places you should target immediately with your resume and try and organize a personal interview if at all possible if you are to land your first job in the film and/or television industry.

All three are outlined below.

The State Film Office

First and foremost, you should get a copy of your resume to your is your state film commission (also known as state film office).

State film commissions, which go by various names, depending on the state you're in, are generally branches of the state government. Often, they are associated with the governor's office. In some states, they are associated with the state government's department of economic development or department of revenue, of the state's department of tourism. They are almost always in the state's capital city.

These commissions, government departments, really, are created to help promote the state. There are few things that helps promote a state as much as a major motion picture or television series being filmed there, then shown nationwide or worldwide to interested audiences.

Before I explain anything more about state film commissions, it is important that you understand why these government departments are so incredibly important to your future employment in the film industry. Film production companies are like travelling circuses (more so than you might suspect). When they come to your state to film the Great American Movie, they are being funded by production companies that are usually based in New York or Los Angeles, and hence bring money into the state from outside. Because the producers and production managers associated these films often know little about shooting regulations in your state or need help figuring out locations for their production, they generally contact your state's film commission for aid.

While the Great American Movie producer gets help with various aspects of his film from the state film office, the state, in return, gets advertising for the state, as well as, on most shoots, the opportunity to recommend some residents of the state for employment on the film crew. This is why the state film commission is your first link to getting a job in the film industry.

In some states, like Florida, the state has created a public-private partnership, in which the state subcontracts the work out to a private company or organization which does the work of the former state film commission.

Unfortunately, sometimes these organizations are not run as well as film commisions run directly by the state, as the motive for profit plays a roll in their operations. In other cases these privately run offices are better than a state run office because they are not mired down with bureacracy.

If you can, try and schedule an interview or meeting with a representative of your state film commission. More than likely, you'll be turned down and told to simply submit a resume to the office, but try and meet the representatives of the office any way you can. When a big movie comes to town, and the producer needs 50 production assistants, it's possible the state film commission might recommend you if you've made a good impression.

One important thing to remember: Your goal is not to try and get a job with the state film commission. You are contacting the state film commission because they are in touch with producers and film companies that are shooting in your state, or planning to come to your state to shoot. Your reason for contacting the state film commission is to tap into their knowledge of what's going on in the film industry locally, and how you can apply for jobs with film and television production companies.

The most important information about state film commissions — their addresses and telephone numbers — appears in Appendix B at the back of the book.

For most states, there is only one state film commission or office. However, in many states that host a lot of film and television production work, there are multiple offices that promote and have information on film and television production.

In California, for example, there are dozens of film commissions, all of which are associated with local governments. The biggest of these offices is, of course, the Los Angeles County Film Office, where the bulk of the world's films and television programs are produced.

Because they are county offices doesn't mean they are small scale, homely institutions. Some county film commissions and offices in California, Florida and other states are busier than the state film commissions in North Dakota and Alaska.

It is important to remember that state film offices, even though linked to the state government, frequently see their phone numbers changed. Between the first draft of this book and the final draft, 35 state film offices changed their telephone numbers! If the telephone numbers listed in Appendix B go out of date, state film offices can very often be found in the yellow pages for your capital city. If not, they can usually be found by calling directory information.

As mentioned, the names given to these offices vary widely. Most are called the state film "office" or the state film "commission." You may have to do some calling around to find the department itself. Try both your state government as well as general telephone directory information. If you describe what office you're looking for, you will get the number eventually.

Upon calling the state film commission in the state in which you're looking for film production information, you must be very careful not to get on the bad side of these people. After you have worked several freelance film projects, the people who work at the state film office may be calling you to tell you about film employment opportunities that are approaching. It would be in your best interest to start and maintain a good working relationship with your state film office.

The first time I called one of these places I simply asked if they had any jobs. They said no, and, not surprisingly, hung up. What I eventually realized was to state the truth, but a little more specifically.

The question I subsequently asked is: "Hi, my name is Cameron Burns and I'm a freelance production assistant (or gaffer, or whatever you do in the film business) and I was wondering if you could tell me about any present or future productions in the state."

What the film commission person will tell you will probably be something like one of the following statements:

1. "Sorry, there are no productions currently shooting in the state, and there are none expected for a while."

2. "There is currently a film being shot in Capitol City (or wherever it's taking place) and the production office phone number is: 123-456-7890."

3. "There are currently no films being shot in the state, but next month we expect two productions to come to the state. They have not set up a production office yet so I don't have any place for you to send a resume or deliver one to."

These responses are pretty standard fare for a state film commission to give you, depending on what's going on in your state. But if you can, talk to these people. They are generally very friendly and helpful and if they know that you're a reputable person looking for work, it's more than likely they'll try to help you in some way.

I must stress that when you make inquiries be very polite, and it's best if you know what type of job you're trying to get on a film. If you've never worked on a film crew, the best position to apply for, no matter what your age, is production assistant (see Chapter 4: Starting Out). That way you can usually get to do a little bit of everything, and, at the same time you'll be able to watch what all the other crew members are doing. When the next film comes to town, you'll know what kinds of positions you are interested in.

Another thing to remember: State film offices are supported by taxpayers. It is your right to call and ask the people in these offices about film production in your state (or other states) — they are public servants. I've seen many state film office representatives get angry at responding to questions from film crew hopefuls, which is appalling! Remember, you pay their salaries. These people work for you.

That said, the other thing to remember is that state film commision offices are not employment agencies. The individuals who work in these offices are on a mission to promote the state, in this case by helping producers and production companies feature their state in films and television programs. Telling you about upcoming productions and potential jobs on film crews is not their job either, but if you use the correct, polite approach, they can tell you about potential jobs.

Other Film Commisions

As mentioned above, many states have more than one film commission. In some states, county and municipal governments have created their own film "commissions" to promote filmmaking within their jurisdiction. These commissions are often a commission in name only. Indeed, some tiny county and city governments might have one government staffer who works part-time as a representative to the film industry. Often, they have no real commission or film office at all, and the liason to the film industry is a representative of the local chamber of commerce or convention center or visitor's bureau. If you can, talk to these people. They often know if a big production is coming to a local area and if you show interest, they can recommend you when a producer is looking for local crew members.

There is an organization called the Association of Film Commissions International (AFCI), with which you should familiarize yourself. This organization includes town governments, city governments, county governments and state governments around the world who are members of its organization. These people are well connected to the film industry, and generally know of productions that are coming to their area.

For example, while Appendix B at the back of this book lists state film commissions for the U.S. and Canada, there are dozens of local film commissions throughout every state who represent their area when the Great American Movie comes to town. Contact these offices, and they can also help you find out about production companies (and therefore jobs) that might be coming to your area. The best way to know what local governments are tuned into filmmakihng, is to check out the AFCI's web page, on the Internet, at: http://www.afciweb.org/m.shtml.

It is important to remember that although these small local commissions and film offices are friendlier and easier to contact and talk with, they are usually less equipped to help you find production work than your state film commission.

Local and State Film and Television Production Companies & Production Handbooks

Every state in the nation has its own film and television industry. The people working in the industry are often a tight-knit group, and control much of the hiring of workers for film and television shoots when one is occuring within

The tools for getting started in Hollywood. Photo by Lefty Angus Burns.

the state. Usually, these communities of film professionals are located in the state's capitol city, and base their operations from that city.

In Denver, for example, a tight-knit community of production professionals exist. They range from directors to sound recordists, and when a large Hollywood movie comes to Colorado, often the professionals in Denver are hired to work on the film, even if it is shot all the way across the state in Grand Junction.

Likewise, some cities control production for a region that might include several states. In the southeast, for example, a film to be shot in, Kentucky, for example, will likely see the bulk of its crew hired from the Atlanta area because Atlanta has the large number of production professionals required for a film shoot.

The reason for this is pure economics. Atlanta has a film and television production industry big enough to survive on its own — shooting Atlanta television commercials, documentaries and the like — whereas Kentucky really doesn't.

Meeting the professionals in your state or city is extremely important. More than any other source, they will be the ones who get to know you, learn how well you work at a particular task, and call you when a film is being shot and they need an employee.

There are many ways to meet these people. However, there will be so many of them in your city or state that the best thing to do is narrow the field before sending them your resume. This means deciding whether you want to work in production administration, with cameras, in video, or in some other type of film work before sending off your resume. It doesn't matter too much if you decide later you'd rather do something else. Career changes within the film and television industry are almost constant.

Perhaps the best way to reach professionals in the film and television industry in your state is to acquire your state's production handbook. These books, which go by various titles, list all the film and television industry professionals and services within your state. They list everything, from directors and producers to special effects artists to wranglers who have horses for hire for film and television shoots.

Generally, production handbooks are put together by state film commissions, to help promote the the film and television industry within the state, and to attract large productions from out of state. Sometimes, they are put together by private publishers. Occasionally, the handbooks are free; generally, there is a fee for the books. The books are generally published each year, so they contain fairly current and accurate information.

To obtain a copy of one, contact your state film commission. Officials there will be able to help you acquire the handbooks, either directly through their offices, or by putting you in touch with the publisher who prints the books.

Once you have your state's production handbook, you will be able to flip through it and see who you might be interested in contacting about work.

Out-of-state Production Companies Shooting in Your Area

The third most important source for work in the the film and television industry is out-of-state production companies shooting in your area. (See "The State Film Commission" above.)

These companies, which shoot advertisements, Hollywood feature films, or television series, are usually small, temporary companies set up by bigger film and television production companies. A large film corporation like Paramount, for example, will create a smaller company that will actually make the film. The names of the smaller companies are often just the name of the film itself. Generally, these companies will only exist in your state or city for the duration of the actual shooting. And, you will rarely find information about how to contact these companies in any published lists.

There are numerous ways to get information about these companies shooting in your state or area.

The state film commission (described above) is one source, however, there are several others, which will be outlined in the next chapter.

Film Job Fact: In the early part of the 20th Century, actor and filmmaker Charlie Chaplin built houses for employees of a film studio he owned in West Hollywood. In 1997, a studio apartment in West Hollywood was going for $800-1,200 per month.

A grip wrangling cameras. Photo by Cameron M. Burns.

Chapter 6
WHO ELSE IS HIRING AND HOW TO CONTACT THEM

While your state film office is probably the best way to find out about film and television productions being shot in your area, there are numerous ways to find out what is going on in the industry, what movie productions are coming to town and how to contact the producers or production managers without going through a government office.

The best sources of information are outlined here.

Film production hotlines

Film production hotlines are a relatively new phenomenon in the film and television industry. Simply put, they are telephone numbers where anyone interested in film and television work can call to find out about what productions are coming to the state or city in which you live.

When you call, you will hear a recorded message with all sorts of information. Some hotlines merely list productions that are in progress and productions that are expected to come to your state. Others list all sorts of other information, from upcoming lectures on filmmaking to web sites related to the film industry.

Almost every state in the Union now has a film production hotline. Most of the hotlines are associated with the state film office, but some — Alaska's, for example — are set up by independent groups of film and television professionals and industry representatives.

Before you try anything else I've advocated or will advocate in this book, pick up your phone and try call one of the many film production hotlines in the United States. You'll be surprised at how accessible the film industry really is.

As mentioned, many of these hotlines list events related to the filmmaking community in your area, from upcoming film festivals to pertinent university courses. Even if the hotline lists no films in production, you might consider attending events listed on the hotlines as often you can meet film industry professionals in your area at these events.

Most, but not all, will list productions that have come to your state. If current productions are on the hotline, the recording will usually list the film's name, producer or production manager. The most important part of these recorded messages is the address and phone numbers of the production offices.

Write these phone numbers down! These people are your potential employers.

Quite often the message will tell you that the production company does not accept "drop-offs". This means that you can't go and visit the production office and introduce yourself or meet any of the people involved with the film. It means you'll have to send your resume by mail. Although this may reduce your chances of getting hired, do it anyway. Then follow up with phone calls to the Production Manager if you can get the phone number.

If there are no films in production or on the way in your particular state, call around to neighboring states. If you live in Utah, call Colorado, Arizona and Nevada. If you live in Georgia, call Florida, Alabama, South Carolina and Tennessee. Call all over the country if you can. The more you find out about what's going on in film production, the better your chances will be of making contact with one of the production companies out there.

The most important information about film production hotlines — an actual list of them for the entire nation — is included in Appendix B at the back of the book.

Trade magazines

Trade magazines are exactly what the names implies — magazines about the trade. There are many magazines devoted to the film and television industry, but there are only a few that can help you find out about film production companies coming to your area.

The main reason you should keep an eye on the trade magazines is because state film offices and local film and television professionals in your area won't know everything that is coming to your area to be shot.

Regularly, trade magazines have information out of Hollywood — the horse's mouth, so to speak — that is being circulated long before the state and local film industry knows that a production is being planned for your area.

Perhaps the two best magazines for this sort of thing are The Hollywood Reporter and Variety.

Both The Hollywood Reporter and Variety include one of the most valuable pieces of information that a film industry employee can ever find, production charts or boards. Production charts in these magazines list films that are currently being produced in the United States and abroad. They list the film's director, producer, production manager and cinematographer. Some of the films listed include telephone numbers and addresses of their production offices. You can use this information to apply for jobs. Addresses for the Hollywood Reporter and Variety are in Appendix C, at the back of the book.

Both the Hollywood Reporter and Variety are published on a daily basis, and both have a larger weekly edition. They are available by subscription for one year or six months. The weekly Hollywood Reporter which is published every Tuesday, includes production charts, and listings of film and television shows shooting all over the world.

If you can afford it, I highly recommend getting a subscription to one or both of these magazines. I recommend The Hollywood Reporter over Variety, but if you can afford it, get both.

Besides the Hollywood Reporter and Variety, there are many local and regional magazines devoted to the film industry across the country.

Web sites

The worldwide web is quickly becoming one of the best places to look for jobs in the film and television industry.

Indeed, some communities of professional production personel have created their own web pages to update those in the industry about what is going on in their area, and how to apply for jobs with various film and television production companies.

In Appendix D at the back of this book are a number of websites that list jobs in the film and television industry. Remember that websites come and go, and website address chage frequently. Try conducting your own search on the web for film industry related sites, using key words like "film," "industry" and "job."

Film Job Fact: 100,000 Canadians work directly in the film industry. The Canadian film industry has been estimated at $2 billion per year.

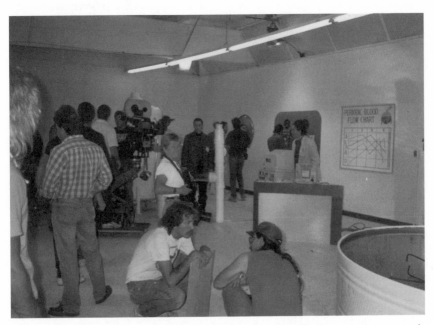

The average film set provides ample opportunity to meet your colleagues. Photo by Cameron M. Burns.

Chapter 7
PERSONAL CONTACTS & NETWORKING

Okay. So maybe you've dropped off a resume at a Production Office, or you've sent one by mail because you're applying for a crew job in a neighboring state. You're probably wondering what else you can do to promote your new career as a film crew technician.

Well, the best thing to do is make personal contact with the Production Manager. Although they are not always solely responsible for hiring Production Assistants, they often can employ a P.A. if they feel that one is needed. If another crew member wants to hire a P.A. to work for their department, they have to get it approved by the Production Manager. When I worked on my first film, I was straight out of college and had been given the number of a film in pre-production in Kentucky by my boss in Research. She didn't know the P.M., and he didn't know me, so I was basically starting from scratch.

I called him several times, as I mentioned earlier, and he talked over a few things with me on the phone. He asked me how old I was, where I went to college, if I had ever worked on a film set before (the answer I gave was no), and numerous other questions. The key to getting the job, I think was telling him that I was very eager to work in the film industry and that I'd do anything to get a job. "I just want to work," I told him repeatedly. I told him that I had many personal references that he could refer to, and that I was willing to relocate to work on his movie.

Personal contact, such as I had with this Production Manager is something that is invaluable in helping your chances of getting hired on a film crew. Personal contact with anyone associated with the film industry is the single most important way of getting into the film industry! If a Production Manager can see that you are a personable individual, that you are not some kind of weird film groupy wanting to gawk at a few stars, and that you're dedicated to a career in the film industry, he will be most sympathetic and therefore more apt to hire you than someone with less ambition. Believe me, some of the people who get hired on film crews are complete flakes, and if you can express to the P.M. that you're a normal intelligent person (with, perhaps, a college degree), and that you are eager to work hard and make a career for yourself, they usually take note of you.

Also, if you live near the Production Office, it is always better to drop off a resume in person. Be prepared to be treated very impolitely (unfortunately film people are very impolite 99% of the time) but if you can manage to just get a few minutes with the P.M., be polite and courteous and straight to the point. Before you go to visit the Production Office, call and ask if the P.M. is there and ask if you can just drop a resume by and say hello to him. It is more likely that you will not even get to meet the P.M., and that your resume will be taken by the Production Coordinator or the Assistant Production Coordinator, but it is definitely worth a shot. Just shaking hands with the P.M. can improve your chances of getting a job.

Also, the people who are in the Production Office when you drop your resume by will probably not appreciate your sticking around too long. As I've said, all sorts of weirdos tend to hang around when a film is starting up. But say hello to anyone else you meet around the office if you can. It's quite probable that you'll bump into a grip or camera assistant, or maybe you'll meet the D.P. or director. You never know. And, if you can just have a short conversation with someone already on a film crew, it may better your chances of getting hired. I once got a job on a film crew because I met the Key Grip in the Production Office. He liked my personality, and quirky sense of humor, so he hired me as a Grip on the spot. I didn't even have to meet the Production Manager.

Also, I suggest you get some business cards made up, even if you're not sure what it is you'd like to do. All you need to get printed on a business card is:

1. Your Name
2. Your Telephone Number
3. "Film Production"

The generic label "Film Production" lets people know that you work in the movies, more importantly in production, but it's not so specific that it labels you as a grip, or electrician or an assistant director. Sometimes you can be overlooked for an electrician position on a film crew because you have a business card that says you work as an assistant director.

Tell the people you give your cards to that you'd like to do whatever their hiring for, even if you don't have any experience in that area. Don't lie, though. If you don't know anything about being an A.D., tell the truth. But also tell the interested person that you would really like to get into "A.D.ing".

I had a friend in Hollywood who worked on big feature films as a grip, because the money was good, but he also worked as a unit production manager on very cheap horror movies. He wanted his resume to read "UPM", but he also wanted the money from working on big budget features as a grip. He passed out his business card to everyone, no matter what job he was going after.

Perhaps after you've worked on several movies and you've got a good idea about what job you like doing, then you can get more business cards printed promoting yourself in your chosen line of work.

Another way to meet people in "show business" is to find out where a film is being shot. Usually the day-to-day location of film production is pretty hush-hush because the last thing a director needs is hundreds of spectators watching him make a movie. But if you can somehow find out, it would be worth your while to get as close to the action as possible.

Watch the newspapers in your area for stories such as, "Hollywood Comes To Town" or "Movie Magic Being Made Locally". Newspapers tend to sell a lot of copies when anything related to the movie industry is printed within their pages.

Listen to the local news on television, also. Sometimes regional stations will report if a Production Company has moved to your area to start shooting a film.

And, if you hear friends, neighbors or acquaintances talking about film production, get involved with the conversation. The more you can find out, and the more you can let people know that you'd like to work in the movie industry, the more chance you have for success.

I worked on a film once where a high school kid rode past the set everyday on his bicycle. He would stop, talk to some of the electricians, watch some of the filming, then continue home. After about a week of this, the best boy electrician asked him if he wanted to work as an Electrician P.A., rolling up large sections of cable and lugging lights around. He took the job, low paying as it was, and continued on in the film industry long after he graduated from high school. The fact was that his personal contact with the electricians got him the job.

So the whole point to this section is that you should, whenever possible, make contact with film crew personnel. They will be able to get a good idea of what you're like, whether they think you would work well as a team and many other things that may land you a position on a film crew.

Film Job Fact: In 1987, the number of movie tickets sold in the U.S. was 1 billion. In 1996, the number was 1.3 billion.

Gang members spray painting grafitti on the set of "Angel Town," South Central Los Angeles, 1989. The gang members, who live in the neighborhood, saw the film crew making a "gang" movie, and were hired to add authentic graffitti to the set. They landed this particular job simply by "cruising." Photo by Cameron M. Burns.

Chapter 8
MAINTAINING A STEADY FLOW OF WORK

Perhaps you've just finished working on your first film. It was a lot of work, but you found it rewarding, and always very interesting. The shooting has ended and you're once again unemployed. What can you do to ensure you get another job?

Show Off?

Well, there are a few things about your second film job that you should know long before you begin working on your first film. In short, your first film job is a chance to showcase yourself, your personality, your work ethic and other idiosynchrasies.

Whether they look like it or not, everyone on a film, especially your first film, is a potential future employer. From the bearded grip who spends his day playing around with sand bags to the slick producer who brings paychecks out to the set, almost anyone can wind up on a film two months later needing to hire other film production personnel like you.

If you don't work extremely hard to make a good impression on your first film job, you might as well plan on getting out of the business.

Likewise, every film you work on will become a showcase of your talents and capabilities, and as long as you show your colleagues you can do the job quickly and efficiently, you will likely be working on movies long into the future.

Crew Listings

When most films and large television productions wrap (finish shooting), the producers or production manager will have a crew list put together. Crew lists are exactly what they sound like: lists of everyone who worked on the production. The list usually includes a worker's address, phone number and other pertinent information. They are created so that film production personnel can stay in touch with one another. If the gaffer liked the way a particular electrician worked, he might want to hire him for the next production the gaffer works on.

It is really important after your first shoot that you be on the crew list if one is made. Sometimes, those right at the bottom of the crew are left off the list. So, a week or two before your first film is scheduled to wrap, ask the pro-

51

duction manager or production coordinator if a crew list will be put together and ask them to include you on the list.

If no crew list is being compiled, try to make your own little crew list. Don't bother putting absolutely everyone on the list — try to include those who you got along with and who obviously liked you. These people are more likely to hire you on future films than those who weren't even sure of your existence on the set.

Business Cards, Business Cards

Business cards are always a good idea. Get some made before you begin working on your first film, so you can hand them out while your on the set. (For more information on business cards, see Personal Contacts and Networking in Chapter 7). Remember, you will be creating impressions, good and bad, on your first film, and it's important to give anyone you think you've made a good impression on one of your cards.

The Inevitale Move to L.A.

It is possible to have a film career anywhere in the country, but if you really want to work a lot, you'll have to consider moving to Los Angeles at some point. L.A. produces something like 90 percent of the world's movies and television programs, and the amount of film industry work there is phenomenal. If you stay in your home state, it may be months before another movie comes to your area.

But be warned, just moving to L.A. can be a problem in itself. If you move there but still don't have any contacts, you'll be unemployed there. It's cheaper to be unemployed in other places; Los Angeles is no city to be broke in, but it's also the place to be if you want to make movies.

When you finish working on your first film, let everyone on the crew know that you are planning to move to L.A. and that you'll probably call them and ask them about work once you get there.

One trick is to try and rent a room from someone on the crew you are working with. This sounds crazy, but can work incredibly well.

By sharing a house or apartment with someone already well-established in the film industry, you will likely be able to ask them for information on upcoming film productions, and even ask if they need any help on their next shoot. After all, the person your renting from is as interested in keeping you employed as you are. He needs your rent!

I did this in 1989. I was living in Moab, Utah, and asked several people on a crew I was working with if anyone had a room they could rent out because I wanted to move to L.A. I moved into a rented a room in a grip's house in the San Fernando Valley, and from that point on, never lacked work. Often my roommate would hire me as an extra grip, or many times he'd refer me to someone who had wanted to hire him, but found him busy on a different film. And I didn't only work as a grip. Because I was busy going from film to film, I found all sorts of other jobs that I wouldn't have found if I was not working on a set everyday.

Whatever the case, the fact that I was living with someone already established in the film industry opened up all sorts of doors for me. Once you're in L.A. and share living quarters with established film production personnel, your career will blossom.

Cruising L.A.?

Another thing that can bring you work is cruising around L.A.. That's right, cruising!

Many production companies shoot all or parts of films on the street in L.A. Often, you can wander up to crew members on these productions and start an idle conversation about the film they are working on. Many crew members love bragging about being in "The Business." If you make a good impression, you can leave a business card or resume with one or several people on that crew. More importantly, find out where the production company they are working for is located, then take your resume to that company's office.

This might sound like a crazy way to get a job, but I have seen dozens of people get hired on film crews simply by showing up on a set or at a production office.

One important thing to remember about streetside contact like this: Don't get in the way. If the crew is busy, under a lot of stress to get the day's shooting completed or otherwise incapacitated, don't hassle them. They'll remember you and make a point of not hiring you for anything if you get in the way.

Film Job Fact: In the film "Annie Hall", actress Diane Keaton's character defended L.A. culture.

Students working on a short film project, UCLA, 1987. Photo by Cameron M. Burns.

Chapter 9
UNIVERSITY OPPORTUNITIES

Universities and colleges throughout the United States offer perhaps some of the greatest opportunities for you to get your foot in the door of the American Film Industry. As I related to you earlier, I got an exceptional start in the movies because I pursued University Internship programs. It gave me a lot of experience and was of importance when later employers came to look at my resume. Although my resume still wasn't anything compared to personal contacts.

Perhaps you aren't currently enrolled in university, though? That's okay. Find out the school nearest to you that has a film studies program. See if you can take night classes, or fit a regular film production class into your schedule. The important thing, however, is that you take classes in film production, rather than film criticism, film history or any other film related topics. Unfortunately fewer schools offer film production than film criticism and history, but try to find one that does offer production.

Once you're in the class you will be working making films with many other students. You will make friends, and, if you stick with the film industry long enough, you'll probably end up working on real movies with some of these people.

Once you're in a Film Production class, start asking around, amongst the professors, about student work-study positions within the film department. Talk to your professor about working in the University Film Department. See if he might have any type of job that you could apply for. Remember, persistence is the key. You may not get a job immediately, but keep after it. Eventually you will.

Also, ask your teacher about university internships in the film industry. This can often be your best way to Hollywood. You will be working for no money, but you'll gain an incredible amount of experience, not to mention an impeccable list of contacts. It's more than likely that people you work with will be calling you because they want to hire you especially if you show an eagerness to work. Ask your professor about an internship program.

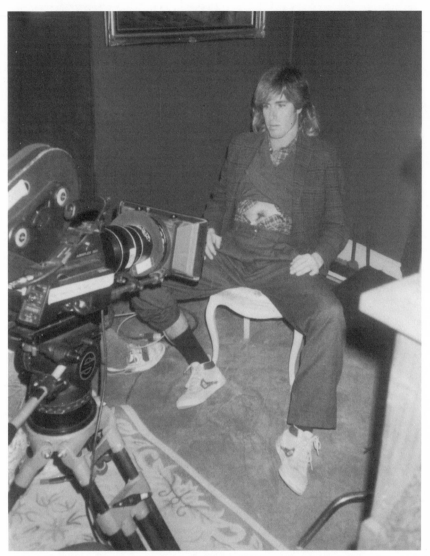

A production assistant showing off his positive attitude by letting the special effects crew use his stomach for a close up during the filming of a cheap horror film. Photo by Cameron M. Burns.

Chapter 10
ATTITUDE & PERSISTENCE

It's hard, when you're starting out to let people know that you're capable, without sounding cocky. Unfortunately, you'll probably end up just keeping your mouth shut and have to do some really awful jobs.

That's okay. Believe me, most people in power in Hollywood started out doing some pretty low-down jobs. Through sheer willingness and good attitude about doing what they were told, they eventually rose to the top.

Try to remember that everything you learn will benefit you in the long run. Smile and be courteous, even if you'd rather punch your boss in the nose.

And, of course, you will get nowhere in the film business if you are not persistent. Quite simply, this is the truth.

You might call 100 people a week to ask about a position on a film crew and have no luck whatsoever in finding a job. Don't worry. The more this happens to you, the more you'll get used to it and, hopefully, the more determined you'll become.

Sometimes it will seem as though there is nothing else you can do to get a film job, when suddenly, out of the blue, you'll get as phone call and you will have landed a job. The only thing you can try to do when you can't find work is keep looking. If you don't persist, you'll get nowhere.

A typical day on the set. Photo by Cameron M. Burns.

APPENDIX A
FILM CREW POSITIONS

Having spent many years crewing films, I have been asked innumerable times: "What's a gaffer?" or "What's does a grip do?" by friends, family and acquaintances. Due to years of such questioning, I have included a gazetteer, a list of who's who on a film crew. Remember that every single film crew is different and that the tasks performed by the various film crew members can be very different from production to production.

Executive Producer

The Executive Producer is the person who finds the money for a film. He either sells the idea to a studio, which then gives him the money with which he can make the movie. Usually Executive Producers simply stick to selling the idea of a film to a studio or financial investor, while the actual day-to-day mechanics of shooting a movie are performed by the Producer or Production Manager. Sometimes, Executive Producers are just very wealthy people who produce the film with their own money.

Producer

This person is usually hired by the Executive Producer, given the major portion of money that the Executive received from the studio, and is then required to make a movie with that money. Often, if the Producer makes the movie for less than the amount he was given, he gets to keep the remaining money, or part of it, and, if the film goes "over budget" it simply means that the Producer couldn't make the film for the amount of money he was given and had to ask the Executive Producer for more. The Executive can do two things if the film goes "over budget". He can spend some of the money he already skimmed off the top, or, more likely, he can go back to the studio and ask for more cash. Executive Producers are very powerful people.

Director

The director of a film can have many different jobs. Primarily, a director decides the way in which scenes are going to be acted. There are about a million different ways to shoot the same piece of dialogue or action and it is the director's job to choose the correct method of portraying that piece of dialogue or action so that it fits into the context of the story.

Secondly, and perhaps more importantly in the case of low-budget films, the director's job is making sure that the film is shot. Everyday, during shooting the director should be moving the technical people on to the next shot, explaining what the action will be and how he'd like to film it. I have worked with many wanna-be directors who think that their job is a purely creative and artistic affair. That is not true. If the director doesn't move the entire crew on to the next shot, the day's filming might not be completed, and, if that happens, it's highly likely that the film will run over budget.

First Assistant Director

Some people say that the hardest job on a film crew is that of first assistant director. Unfortunately, for the first A.D., it's true. They are the "policemen and managers" of the film set. They organize everyone so that when the director, actors and technical crew are all ready to shoot a scene everything will come together at the exact same time. For instance, often the director will be ready to direct, the actors will be ready to act, the technical crew will be ready, but the actors make-up hasn't been put on. The first A.D. often gets blamed for slip-ups such as this. Basically they are conductors and the entire film crew are like musicians.

The first A.D. is also required to perform "sound lock-up", which basically means organizing all the other A.D.s to help him quiet the set and surrounding area. He even has to tell people to shut up other crew members who are making noise.

Also, the first A.D usually directs the extras who make up part of crowd scenes.

Second Assistant Director

Like the first A.D., this person works controlling the sound of a movie. But he performs a few jobs for the first A.D. who usually has to stay at the director's side throughout the day. For instance, he is also in charge of making sure that the actors are taken care of, and ready when they need to be. They have to make sure that one of the drivers will pick up the actor when that actor is needed and driven to the set. He makes sure that the actors are delivered safely to their hotels at night.

Also, he is responsible for keeping track of most of the contractual agreements and paper work (such as W-4 forms) between the production company and crew members.

Second Second Assistant Director

The second second assistant director is a junior version of the second assistant director and often takes on half the second A.D.'s workload. This is true especially when a film has many large and involved crowd scenes. The second A.D. will be required to direct many of the extras while the second second A.D. will takeover all the contractual and "actor service" jobs. Sometimes a film's producer will hire a second second A.D. if the shooting locations are complicated and require that the second A.D. work with the first A.D. performing sound control and set security.

Cinematographer

The cinematographer or director of photography, or D.P. as they're more commonly known, is the head of the entire technical crew of the film. The technical crew are the electricians, gaffers, grips and other people who deal with the lighting or photography of a film.

However, what the D.P. is principally known for is the actual photography of the action, whether it be a car exploding or two lovers kissing. Once the director has told the D.P. what he is looking for, the D.P. decides which lights should be used, how the camera should be set up to record the actors, what lenses would work best, which light effects are best for each particular shot, and so on. The director and D.P., you will find, confer about much of the photography of a film.

Camera Operator

On low-budget films, the camera operator and the D.P. are often one and the same. However, on bigger films (usually $3 million or more) there is a D.P. and a camera operator. Also, it is not uncommon for the D.P. to leave all the "lens work" to the camera operator, and the D.P. may never look through the lens during an entire film production. This leaves the camera operator to line up actors upon their marks and ascertain that the entire scene is within the camera's frame. On many films the camera operator does nothing except sit upon a dolly, look through the lens and switch the camera on when the first A.D. says roll film.

First Assistant Cameraman

The first assistant cameraman does basically two things: "rack" focus (focus the camera for the camera operator) and change lenses when the D.P. asks for a lens change.

Although most camera assistants wish to one day D.P. a film, it is common to find first assistants who do nothing their entire film career except "pull" focus, as it is also called. I knew one fellow who had been a first assistant for 20 years. He said he loved being a first assistant because it was such a technical job. He said he never wanted to operate the camera or D.P. a film in his life, although he had been offered those positions.

Second Assistant Cameraman

The second assistant cameraman loads the magazines of film that will be shot during the film. These devoted camera assistants spend much of the day in the camera crew's truck, which usually has a built in darkroom, loading and downloading magazines of film. You will see them running between the truck and the camera bringing fresh film once the present magazine has been used. They also are in charge of retrieving new lenses from the camera truck when the D.P. asks for a lens change. And, they have the mathematical task of keeping track of all the film shot during the day, ordering new film if needed and reporting to the production manager just how much film has been used. They are also the people you see standing in front of the camera with the slate or clapboard that marks the beginning of each take.

Gaffer

The gaffer is in charge of all the lighting and electrical requirements on a film set. He works directly under the cinematographer, and translates the D.P.s ideas about illuminating a scene into the actual individual lights.

Before a scene is shot, and often before the film production commences at all, the D.P. will give the gaffer a brief run through of what he's looking for as far as lighting each scene. It's the gaffer's job to then decide whether a 1 kiloWatt light should be placed behind an actors head, or a 5 kiloWatt light. Sometimes the D.P. will even suggest certain lights go in certain places, however picking the exact light is usually left for the gaffer.

Also, the gaffer, although he is not required, usually becomes responsible for the electricity supply to the set, especially if the film is being shot at a remote location, where a generator is required. The gaffer often has to organize lighting and electricity for the make-up and wardrobe trailers, the actors trailer, craft service and various other crew members who want power. He often relies on a generator operator, someone who simply runs a portable electrical generator, to help him achieve this.

Best Boy

A best boy can belong to the electrical department, and therefore work for the Gaffer, or he can be one of the grips and work under the key grip. Often, to make the distinction you may hear best boys referred to as "Best Boy Grip", or "Best Boy Electric".

A best boy is a gaffer's (or key grip's) right hand man. He is responsible for ascertaining that all the electrical equipment is returned to the truck (or set) at night. He is responsible for making sure that any rented equipment is returned to the rental company at the close of the production, not to mention any paperwork that accompanies the equipment. And he is usually responsible for renting extra equipment, usually lights, that the electricians might need.

A best boy is also responsible for the paperwork (W-4 forms, production contracts) of the members of his department (the electricians or the grips) including the head of the department (the gaffer or key grip).

Electrician

An electrician works for the gaffer and sets up an electrical infrastructure around the set. From the enormous generator that is usually several hundred yards from the set, the electrician lays down hundreds of feet of cable that will carry either AC or DC (usually AC) current to the set to power lights, recharge the dolly, run coffee makers, even power the hairdresser's blow dryer. If you've ever seen a film set, especially an indoor set, you will have seen this cable running every which way around the set.

Electricians are also responsible for the lights. They can often be seen running from the set to the electrical supply truck retrieving different lights that the gaffer has deemed necessary.

Key Grip

The key grip is head of the grip department. He, like all the grips, is responsible for removing light (see Grip description below). The key, however, makes all the decisions concerning the use of flags, and other light altering devices. He is also the principle person involved in setting up a support system for the camera. He usually lugs the tripods around the set, or, more likely, drives the dolly that the camera is mounted upon. Because he remains with the camera for most of the day, the key grip can be in constant communication with the D.P. who will tell him what light needs alteration before a scene is shot. The DP usually tells the grips and electricians what shot is next so that they can begin setting up equipment far in advance of shooting. This saves time when its comes time to shoot the scene since preparing the lighting equipment generally takes longer than anything else.

Grip

The grips, like the electricians, are responsible for lighting the set before a shoot. However, the major difference between the grips and electricians is that the electricians put the light into a shot, while the grips take it away. Grips are responsible for setting up flags (large pieces of black cloth) and other fabrics that alter the effect of the light.

Grips are also responsible for setting up many of the light-stands used on a shoot. Both the grips and the electricians have light stands, and depending upon the type of stand needed, either a grip or an electrician will set up a stand.

Grips are also required to set up dolly track and push the camera dolly during a tracking (or dollying) shot.

Also, it is interesting to note that grips, although they may set up light stands, are generally not allowed to handle the actual light itself. On a film production where the crew are all union members, this rule is law and the technicalities of it are often hotly contested. On non-union shoots this fine line is not as well preserved.

Swing

A swing is simply someone who works as both an electrician and a grip, depending upon what type of shooting is going on at the time.

These jobs aren't as common as grip or electrician jobs because they usually require that each day the filming requires very different lighting situations. For instance, when the shooting is all outside in the bright sun, there isn't much for an electrician to do. In that case a swing would work as a grip, and when the filming returned to nighttime exteriors, a swing would probably work as an electrician. Swings, electricians, and grips are often derived from the same group of young men who work whichever job they're offered.

Property Master

The property master on a film crew is the person in charge of all the little effects that go into a film set that make it realistic. For example, if a film is set in a bicycle shop, the property master is required to rent or buy all the bikes, bike parts and accessories that make the scene look like a real bike shop. He is also required to find all the tools that would go into a bike shop, all the clamps, shelves, spare tires, and things like that.

However, there is a certain amount of ambiguity between what the property master is required to provide and what the set decorators provide. For example, say there was a film being shot that was meant to take place in a library. It is likely that the property master would not be required to provide the books and shelves; they would be provided by set decorators. He would, however, have to provide books that the actors were actually handling or were featured in the film. (Featured simply means that the viewer can distinguish that particular book when he sees it on the screen).

As with all the positions on a film crew, many of the tasks overlap with those found in other positions.

Production Designer

The production designer is very important to the way a film will look. A production designer (along with the director) makes many of the decisions concerning what a set will look like; which way the couch will face, where the window will be, what color the walls will be, things like that.

His decisions don't only affect interior scenes. How the exterior of a particular house or building will look in the film is also decided by the production designer. The set decorators work under the Production Designer in preparing the set for shooting.

Production Manager

The best way to describe a production manager (also known as a unit production manager, U.P.M. or P.M.) is to call him a "mini-producer". This person is responsible for the day to day running of the office (or clerical) portion of a film crew. If you work on a film crew you will rarely see this person on the set because his work takes place at the production office. He performs all the paperwork that is required to keep a film crew running. He makes sure paychecks get to the crew members. He rents hotel rooms for crew, automobiles for directors and producers; he rents various amenities that top-level crew members indulge in, like refrigerators for hotel rooms, and other things.

He also signs a check if, for instance, the key grip needs to rent another dolly or buy more lumber for a particular dolly shot.

The P.M. does a lot of other tasks, too, like making sure that the actors are picked up at the airport and driven to their hotel.

Production Coordinator

In the same way that the production manager is a mini version of the producer, the production coordinator is a mini version of the production manager. Whereas the P.M. usually decides to rent a hotel room for the producer, it is usually the production coordinator (or assistant production coordinator) who makes the actual phone call to reserve a room. He is usually the one who is responsible for xeroxing the next day's call sheet (the daily schedule of what's being shot).

Basically, to sum it up, the production coordinator implements all the decisions made by the P.M. Sometimes a P.A. or assistant production coordinator may help him, but ultimately it's his task.

Film Job Fact: The word "gaffer" is believed to have come from the word "grandfather." Some historians believe it to be a term of endearment for the old longshoremen who were hired to handle extremely large lights during the film industry's early days.

Preparing dolly track. Photo by Cameron M. Burns.

APPENDIX B
STATE FILM OFFICES

State Film Offices exist throughout the United States. These offices are liaisons between the various states and independent film production companies that wish to shoot in that particular state.

In many states, city, county and even local governments have created their own film commisions. In many cases, these commissions are not full-blown commissions, like those found at the state level. Often, local commissions consist of just one part-time government employee who is the designated local contact for production companies looking to shoot in that area. However, it is often worth contacting these smaller commissions to let them know you live in their area and are interested in working in the film industry.

Ironically, in some of the larger states in terms of production, such as New York and California, the state or city film offices have little or no information about films currently in production. That information is best had through the Hollywood Reporter or Variety.

Remember, be polite, patient and courteous and you'll get the information you want, and, hopefully, a job.

UNITED STATES

ALABAMA
Alabama Film Production Hotline
334-242-4196

Alabama Film Office
401 Adams Ave.
Montgomery, Alabama 36130
334-242-4195
1-800-633-5898
Fax: 334-242-2077

ALASKA
Alaska Film Group Production Hotline
907-566-3664

Alaska Film Office
3601 C Street, Suite 700

Anchorage AL 99503
907-269-8137
Fax: 907-269-8136

ARIZONA
Arizona Film Production Hotline
602-280-1389

Arizona Film Commission
3800 North Central Avenue, Building D
Phoenix, AZ 85012
602-280-1380
1-800-523-6695
Fax: 602-280-1384

ARKANSAS
Arkansas Film Production Hotline
501-682-2397

Arkansas Motion Picture Office
1 State Capitol Mall, Room 2C-200
Little Rock, AK 72201
501-682-7676
Fax: 501-682-FILM (3456)

CALIFORNIA
California Film Commission
7080 Hollywood Boulevard, Suite 900
Hollywood, CA 90028-6126 USA
213-860-2960
800-858-4PIX
FAX: 213-860-2972

Los Angeles County Film Office
(Entertainment Industry Development Corp.)
7083 Hollywood Boulevard, 5th Floor
Hollywood CA 90028
213-957-1000
FAX: 213-962-4966

COLORADO
Colorado Film Production Hotline
303-620-4567

Colorado Film Commission
1625 Broadway, Suite 1700
Denver, CO 80202
303-620-4500

A low budget shoot in Colorado. Photo by Cameron M. Burns.

CONNECTICUT
Connecticut Film Commission
Connecticut Department of Economic Development
505 Hudson Street
Hartford, CT 06106
860-270-8087

DELAWARE
Delaware Development Office
Film Division
99 King's Highway
P.O. Box 1401
Dover DE 19901-7305
302-739-4271

DISTRICT OF COLUMBIA
District of Columbia
Office of Motion Picture and TV Development
717 14th Street NW, 11th Floor
Washington D.C. 20005
202-727-6608
Fax: 202-727-3787

FLORIDA
Florida Entertainment Commission
505 17th Street
Miami Beach, FL 33139 USA
305-673-7468
FAX: 305-673-7168

GEORGIA
Georgia Film Office
P.O. Box 1776
Atlanta, Georgia 30301
285 Peachtree Center Ave., Suite 1000
Atlanta GA 30303
404-656-7836
Fax: 404-651-9063

Georgia Film Production Hotline
404-656-6497

HAWAII
Hawaii Film Office
P.O. Box 2359
Honolulu, HI 96804
808-586-2570
FAX: 808-586-2572

IDAHO
Idaho Film Bureau
700 West State Street
P.O. Box Box 83720
Boise, ID 83720 USA
208-334-2470
800-942-8338
FAX: 208-334-2631

ILLINOIS
Illinois Film Office
100 West Randolph, Suite D-400
Chicago, IL 60601
312-814-3600

Illinois Film Office Production Hotlines
Crew: 312-427-WORK (9675)
Cast: 312-427-FILM (3456)

INDIANA
Indiana Film Commission
1 North Capitol, Suite 700
Indianapolis, IN 46204 USA
317-232-8829
FAX: 317-233-6887

Indiana Film Production Hotline
1-800-879-7998

IOWA
Iowa Film Office
200 East Grand Avenue
Des Moines, IA 50309
515-242-4726
FAX: 515-242-4859

Iowa Film Production Hotline
515-242-4757

KANSAS
Kansas Film Commission
700 SW Harrison Street, Suite 1300
Topeka, KS 66603
785-296-4927
FAX: 785-296-6988

KENTUCKY
Kentucky Film Commission
500 Mero Street, Capitol Plaza Tower, Suite 2200
Frankfort, KY 40601 USA
502-564-3456

800-345-6591
FAX: 502-564-7588

LOUISIANA
Louisiana Film Commission
343 N. 3rd St., Suite 400
Baton Rouge, LA 70802
P.O. Box 44320
Baton Rouge, LA 70804-4320
504-342-8150
FAX: 504-342-7988

Louisiana Film Production Hotline
504-342-FILM (3456)

MAINE
Maine Film Office
59 State House Station
Augusta, Maine 04333
207-287-5703
FAX: 207-287-8070

Maine Film Production Hotline
207-624-7851

MARYLAND
Maryland Film Office
217 E. Redwood Street, 9th Floor
Baltimore, MD 21202 USA
410-767-6340
800-333-6632
FAX: 410-333-0044

Maryland Film Production Hotline
410-767-0067

MASSACHUSSETTS
Massachusetts Film Office
10 Park Plaza, Suite 2310
Boston, MA 2116 USA
617-973-8800
FAX: 617-973-8810

Massachusetts Film Production Hotline
617-973-8800

MICHIGAN
Michigan Film Office
201 North Washington Square, Victor Centre 5th Floor
Lansing, MI 48913 USA
517-373-0638
800-477-3456
FAX: 517-241-0593

MINNESOTA
Minnesota Film Board
401 North 3rd Street, Suite 460
Minneapolis, MN 55401 USA
612-332-6493
FAX: 612-332-3735

Minnesota Film Production Hotline
612-333-0436

MISSISSIPPI
Mississippi Film Office
520 George St.
Jackson, MS 39201
P.O. Box 849
Jackson, MS 39205
601-359-3297
FAX: 601-359-5757

Mississippi Film Production Hotline
601-359-2112

MISSOURI
Missouri Film Office
301 West High Street, Room 720
Jefferson City, MI 65102
P.O. Box 118
Jefferson City, MI 65102
573-751-9050
FAX: 573-751-7384

MONTANA

Montana Film Office
1424 9th Avenue
Helena, MT 59620
406-444-3762
800-553-4563
FAX: 406-444-4191

Montana Film Production Hotline
406-444-3960

On location in Montana. Photo by Cameron M. Burns.

NEBRASKA
Nebraska Film Office
700 South 16th
P.O. Box 94666
Lincoln, NE 68509
402-471-3680
800-228-4307
FAX: 402-471-3026

NEVADA
Nevada Film Commision

555 East Washington, Suite 5400
Las Vegas, NV 89101
702-486-2711
FAX: 702-486-2701

Nevada Film Production Hotline
702-486-2727

NEW HAMPSHIRE
New Hampshire Film Commission
172 Pembroke Road
Concord, NH 03301
P.O. Box 1856
Concord, NH 03302
603-271-2598
FAX: 603-271-6784

NEW JERSEY
New Jersey Motion Picture/TV Commission
153 Halsey Street
Newark, NJ 07101
P.O. Box 47023
Newark, NJ 07101
973-648-6279
FAX: 973-648-7350

NEW MEXICO
New Mexico Film Office
1100 South St. Francis Drive
Santa Fe, NM 87505
P. O. Box 20003
Santa Fe, NM 87504
800-545-9871
505-827-9810
FAX: 505-827-9799

New Mexico Film Production Hotline
505-827-9835

NEW YORK
Mayor's Office of Film, Theater and Broadcasting
(New York City Film Commission)
1697 Broadway, 6th Floor

New York, NY 10019
212-489-6710
FAX: 212-307-6237
(The Mayor's Office has no film production hotline, but offers an automatic fax
back list of films currently in production in New York City. For directions on
using the service, call the office, or dial the fax back service directly at 212-
262-8826. It's difficult to get through.)

New York St. Governor's Office of Motion Picture and Television
Development. (New York State Film Commission.)
633 Third Avenue, 33rd Floor
New York, NY 10017 USA
212-803-2330
FAX: 212-803-2339
(For films in production, contact The Mayor's Office, listed above.)

NORTH CAROLINA
North Carolina Film Office
301 N. Wilmington Street
Raleigh, North Carolina 27601
919-733-9900
FAX: 919-715-0151

North Carolina Film Production Hotline
1-800-232-9227

NORTH DAKOTA
North Dakota Film Commission
Liberty Memorial Building
604 East Boulevard Avenue, 2nd Floor
Bismark ND 58505
800-328-2871
701-328-2525
FAX: 701-328-4878

OHIO
Ohio Film Commission
77 South High Street, 29th Floor
Columbus OH 43266
P.O. Box 1001
Columbus, OH 43266
800-230-3523
614-466-2284

FAX: 614-466-6744

OKLAHOMA
Oklahoma Film Commission
440 South Houston, Suite 304
Tulsa, OK 74127
800-766-3456
918-581-2660
FAX: 918-581-2244

OREGON
Oregon Film Office
121 Southwest Salmon Street, Suite 1205
Portland, OR 97204
503-229-5832
FAX: 503-229-6869

Oregon Film Production Hotline
503-986-0212

PENNSYLVANIA
Pennsylvania Film Office
455 Forum Building
Harrisburg, PA 17120
717-783-3456
FAX: 717-787-0687

Pittsburgh Area Film Production Hotline
412-281-3343

Pittsburgh Area Film Production Hotline
215-686-3663

RHODE ISLAND
Rhode Island Film Commission
25 Dorrance Street
Providence, Rhode Island 02903
401-273-3456
FAX: 401-274-8240

SOUTH CAROLINA
South Carolina Film Office
1205 Pendleton St.

Columbia, SC 29201
P.O. Box 7364
Columbia, SC 29202
803-737-0490
FAX: 803-737-3104

South Carolina Film Production Hotline
800-269-7281 (in-state only)
803-737-3022 (out of state only)

SOUTH DAKOTA
South Dakota Film Commission
711 East Wells Avenue
Pierre, SD 57501
800-952-3625
605-773-3301
FAX: 605-773-3256

South Dakota Film Production Hotline
605-773-5977

TENNESSEE
Tennessee Film, Entertainmnt & Music Commission
320 6th Avenue North, 7th Floor
Nashville, TN 37243
615-741-3456
800-251-8594
FAX: 615-741-5829

TEXAS
Texas Film Commission
1100 San Jacinto, Suite 355
Austin TX 78701
P.O. Box 13246
Austin, TX 78711
512-463-9200
FAX: 512-463-4114

Texas Film Production Hotline
512-463-7799

U.S. VIRGIN ISLANDS
U.S. Virgin Islands Film Promotion Office

P.O. Box 6400
St. Thomas, V.I. 804 USVI
809-775-1444
809-774-8784
FAX: 809-774-4390

Setting up a shot. Photo by Cameron M. Burns.

UTAH
Utah Film Commission
324 South State, Suite 500
Salt Lake City, UT 84111
800-453-8824
801-538-8740
FAX: 801-538-8886
(To get the Utah Film Production Hotline number, call the Utah Film
Commission. It is only given out to Utah residents.)

VERMONT
Vermont Film Commission
10 Baldwin Street
P.O. Box 129
Montpelier VT 05601

802-828-3618

Vermont Film Production Hotline
802-828-3680

VIRGINIA
Virginia Film Production Hotline
(804) 287-5070

Virginia Film Office
901 East Byrd St., 19th Flr.
Richmond, VA 23219
800-854-6233
804-371-8204
FAX: 804-371-8177

Virginia Film Production Hotline
800-641-0810

WASHINGTON
Washington State Film Office
2001 6th Avenue, Suite 2600
Seattle, WA 98121
206-464-7148
FAX: 206-464-7222

Washington Film Production Hotline
(206) 464-6074

WEST VIRGINIA
West Virginia Film Office
State Capital Complex, Building 6, Room 553
Charleston, WV 25305
800-982-3386
304-558-2234
FAX: 304-558-1189

WISCONSIN
Wisconsin Film Office
201 West Washington Avenue, 2nd Floor
Madison, WI 53702
800-345-6947 (ext. 0)
608-267-3456

FAX: 608-266-3403

Wisconsin Film Production Hotline
800-345-6947 (ext. 3)

WYOMING
Wyoming Film Office
I-25 and College Drive
Cheyenne, WY 82002
800-458-6657
307-777-3400
FAX: 307-777-6904

Wyoming Film Production Hotline
307-777-7851 (ext. 1, ext. 1)

CANADA

ALBERTA
Alberta Film Office
639 5th Ave. Southwest, Suite 660
P.O Box 2100, Station M
Calgary, AB T2P 2M5 CANADA
403-221-7868
FAX: 403-221-7857

BRITISH COLUMBIA
British Columbia Film Commission
601 West Cordova Street
Vancouver, BC V6B 1G1 CANADA
604-660-2732
FAX: 604-660-4790

British Columbia Film Production Hotline
604-660-3569

MANITOBA
Manitoba Film & Sound Development Corp.
Suite 333-93 Lombard Avenue
Winnipeg, MB R3B 3B1 CANADA
204-947-2040
FAX: 204-956-5261

NEW BRUNSWICK
Film New Brunswick
770 Main St.
Moncton, NB E1C 1E7 CANADA
506-869-6868
FAX: 506-869-6840

NEWFOUNDLAND
Newfoundland & Labrador Film Development Corp.
197-199 Water Street
St. John's, Newfoundland A1C 1B4 CANADA
709-738-3456 (FILM)
FAX: 709-739-1680

NOVA SCOTIA
Nova Scotia Film Development. Corp./Location Services
1724 Granville Street
Halifax, NS B3J 1X5 CANADA
902-424-7185
FAX: 902-424-0563

ONTARIO
Ontario Film Development Corporation
175 Bloor St. East, Suite 300, North Tower
Toronto, ONT M4W 3R8 CANADA
416-314-6858
FAX: 416-314-6876

Ontario Film Production Hotline
416-314-6877

PRINCE EDWARD ISLAND
Prince Edward Island Film Office
c/o Enterprise PEI
P. O. Box 910
Charlottetown, PEI C1A 7L9 CANADA
902-368-6329
FAX: 902-368-6301

QUEBEC
Montreal Film & Television Commmission
413 Saint-Jacques Street, 4th Floor

Montreal, QUE H2Y 1N9 CANADA
514-872-2883
FAX: 514-872-3409

Quebec City Film Bureau
1126 Chemin St-Louis, #802, Sillery,
Québec G1S 1E5, CANADA
418-681-8232
FAX: 418-681-5215

SASKATCHEWAN
SaskFILM/Locations Saskatchewan
2445 13th Avenue, Suite 340
Regina, Saskatchewan S4P OW1 CANADA
306-347-3456
FAX: 306-359-7768

YUKON
Yukon Film Commisson
P.O. Box 2703
Whitehorse, Yukon Y1A 2C6 CANADA
403-667-5400
FAX: 403-393-6456

Film Job Fact: In the film "Speed," there is a scene in which actor Keanu Reeves' character unhandcuffs a man from the railing of the bus. If you look closely, just before Reeves unhandcuffs the man, you can see a bald head belonging to one of the camera crew, as he hurries to move out of the way. Some camera crew members have been fired for smaller infractions.

Shooting a horse race. Photo by Cameron M. Burns.

APPENDIX C
FILM INDUSTRY TRADE MAGAZINES

There are hundreds of employment magazines, newspapers and tabloids across the country, however, they generally do not list when and where film production is taking place. Although The Hollywood Reporter and Variety do list numerous jobs in the entertainment industry, the vast majority of the jobs these publications list are office-type, permanent jobs in the Los Angeles and New York areas. Still, even taking a desk job in Hollywood might lead to other opportunities in the film industry.

Occaisionally, producers do advertise for crew members in the help wanted sections, and sometimes it is possible to find job placement agencies advertsing in The Hollywood Reporter and Variety.

More important than anything, these publications are good sources for finding out about films in production, which can help you get started looking for a job. Most of the films listed in the production section of the magazines give some indication as to where they are being shot. Once you find a film coming to your part of the country, you can contact your local film office to find out who to get in touch with locally.

The Enteratinment Employment Journal is one of the few publications aimed solely at helping job-seekers in the film and television industry, and can be a good starting point for a job search.

The Hollywood Reporter
6715 Sunset Blvd
Hollywood CA 90028
(213)464-7411

Variety
5700 Wilshire Blvd, Suite 120
Los Angeles CA 90036
(213)857-6600

The Enteratinment Employment Journal
Department 1000W
5632 Van Nuys Blvd. Suite 320
Van Nuys, CA 91401-4600
1-800-335-4335
In CA call: 818-901-6330

The author pointing his finger and pretending to work hard on second unit photography. Photo: Cameron M. Burns collection.

APPENDIX D
RELATED WEBSITES

Web pages come and go frequently, so if you get online to start looking for film industry work, remember to use a search engine to locate appropriate web pages. Try using key words for a search such as "film" and "job."

The following web pages are a few we located shortly before this book went to press. Their exact addresses are likely to change at any time. The current address is followed by a few notes on the individual page.

http://www.wldrse.com/jobs.htm
Wild rose films website, an independent film production company

http://www.mandy.com/3/usajo.html
Mandy's Directory of film industry jobs. This is one of the best pages on the web for finding a film job, or getting in touch with producers and production managers.

http://www.hotwired.com/dreamjobs/96/26/oldpage1a.html
Lists jobs at the National Museum of Photography, Film & Television

http://www-scf.usc.edu/~nott/eec.htm
Entertainment Employment Center: Jobs in television, film, acting, modeling - an "entertainment recource page. Includes jobs for television, film, acting, modeling, commercials." Put together by students and faculty of the University of Southern California.

ScreenSite. This web page caters to those seeking film-related teaching jobs in colleges. It offers both a resume service, where you can post your resume, as well as a job listing, of current positions available in the film and television industry.
The resume service is at:
http://www.sa.ua.edu/TCF/teach/employ/resume.htm
The job listing service is at:
http://www.sa.ua.edu/TCF/teach/employ/

http://www.itvs.org/loop.html
The Independent Television Service (ITVS) lists some jobs, at:

http://www.filmmaker.com/book/gb3.html
Filmmaker.com Guestbook - This is a great place to look for a job (some of which don't pay) to get some experience in the film industry. New messages are added almost daily. Many student films that need help are listed.

http://www.eej.com/
The Entertainment Employment Journal

http://www.floridafilm.com/
The Florida Entertainment Commission

http://Film-Production.info-access.com/

http://www.filmbiz.com/
FilmBiz is a web page created by professionals in the industry where your talents can be posted.

http://www.showbizjobs.com.

Film Job Fact: Many people who work in the film industry have tremendously huge egos.

INDEX

Film Job Fact: The fifth edition of the Oxford Dictionary (U.K.) gives one definition of film as "dimness over the eyes."

Notes

Notes

Notes

Notes

About The Author

Cameron M. Burns grew up in Australia, and moved to the United States in 1978. After earning a degree in architecture from the University of Colorado in 1987, he began working in the film industry. He has worked on feature films, documentaries, television advertisements, and promotional and industrial films and videos throughout the country.

In 1991 he began writing fulltime. He has written extensively for newspapers and magazines throughout the U.S. and abroad, and has authored several non-fiction books.